IMAGES
of England

TYNEMOUTH AND CULLERCOATS

Tynemouth, 1893. A young girl sits and writes a letter.

IMAGES
of England

TYNEMOUTH AND CULLERCOATS

Compiled by
John Alexander

TEMPUS

The Victorian architectural design of Tynemouth station, pictured in 1900, remains to this day.

First published 1999, reprinted 2000, 2001, 2003

Tempus Publishing Limited
The Mill, Brimscombe Port,
Stroud, Gloucestershire, GL5 2QG

British Library Cataloguing in Publication Data.
A catalogue record for this book is available from the British Library.

ISBN 0 7524 1673 1

Typesetting and origination by Tempus Publishing Limited
Printed in Great Britain by Midway Colour Print, Wiltshire

Contents

HMS *Resolution*, as seen from Tynemouth's Collingwood Monument.

Acknowledgements

Contributors include Charles W. Steel (proprietor of Times Past), Raey and Muriel Taylor, Helen and Margaret Williamson, Judy Taylor, Terry and Marion Hall, Harold and Edmund Atkinson, Derek and Janice Short, Dr Stewart Evans and Carol Weiss of The Dove Marine Laboratory, Newcastle University, The Fisherman's Mission, Claire Taylor, Beryl Derbyshire, Joy Weatherson.

Collapsed Cullercoats Pier, 1999.

Introduction

Tynemouth and Cullercoats are steeped in history, reaching back over centuries. However, this is not the place to attempt a thorough account of 700 years of history, suffice it to say that Tynemouth Priory and Castle are two constant reminders of how much time has elapsed since these two great coastal villages were first formed.

This book concentrates on the twentieth century just as we are leaving it. Tynemouth retains much of its heritage, but, alas, Cullercoats has not been so lucky. A massive demolition programme in the 1970s wiped out much of what is termed as 'old Cullercoats'. At the time it was doubtless viewed as 'progress', but, after undertaking research and speaking to people who recall the succession of bulldozers storming in and knocking down their quaint fishing village, the general consensus is one of total dismay that the buildings and streets of old were demolished without any thought of preservation.

Photography was really taking off towards the end of the nineteenth century as postcard makers and families began to buy cameras and capture the scenes around them. Initially it was, in the main – like many new inventions, a hobby for people with more than a few pennies in their pockets. Nevertheless, as you will see throughout this book, the results have given us a unique opportunity to take a look at our community's past – the way it looked and the way that people lived then.

Unlike many books of this kind, a concerted effort was made to not rely on local libraries for archive photographic material, but instead to seek out photographs which had neither been displayed nor even seen the light of day for many years. That is not to say that all the photographs contained within these pages are newly discovered archive material – I dare not make such a claim – however, a fair proportion are.

While just less than ninety photographs were drawn from a private collection owed by Mr Charles Steel, proprietor of Times Past, others were obtained from local residents who had heard of my appeal in the local press. The chapters entitled Marden Farm, Rogues Gallery and Fishwives, and Buildings of Distinction are prime examples of where my quest has been successful; otherwise these photographs would have remained held in private albums to be viewed only by family members and close friends. Instead, they have been made available for all of us to enjoy.

Research was undertaken in the same fashion. I discovered one local history book that was helpful, *Cullercoats, Whitley and Monkseaton*, written in 1893 by William Weaver Tomlinson, and loaned to me by Terry and Marion Hall. Further vital information was uncovered by talking to those elderly people who still have vivid memories of the bygone times of Tynemouth and Cullercoats.

The finished result, therefore, is a book which, although only skimming the surface of the ever-changing faces of Tynemouth and Cullercoats, has honest intentions. While it was my aim to try to include a wide selection of photographs from every decade, it is in reality impossible to do this in just one volume. However, there is always scope to follow up this collection of photographs with a further one, if enough interest is generated.

John Alexander
Summer 1999

One
Marden Farm

John Fenwick Wilson, c. 1903.
John died in 1920, aged sixty-one.
The following photographs were
taken at Marden Farm over a
twenty-four year period, from 1895
to 1919. They show the working
side of the farm, the effect of the
First World War, and much lighter
times; friends of the Wilsons
relaxing, farm workers, servants
and others. Between the war years
of 1914 to 1918, soldiers were
stationed at the farm. It proved to
be a harmonious relationship
which both the farm and the Army
embraced, working together to see
the war through.

Henry Fenwick Wilson, *c.* 1910. The death of Henry Fenwick Wilson MBE at the age of seventy-eight on 14 November 1966, more or less closed the chapter on one of the region's most famous farming families. Marden Farm was situated just off what is now known as the Broadway, between Cullercoats and Tynemouth. It had been under the tenancy of the Wilsons, with the land owned by the Duke of Northumberland, from the 1880s to 1970. Henry had succeeded his father John Fenwick Wilson in 1920, and soon built up, in his own right, a fine reputation as both pillar of the community and as an excellent farmer. However, during the early 1950s an ever-increasing housing programme began to swallow up much of Marden Farm land. In May 1957, Henry was forced to sell some of his cattle to 'make room for more houses'. At the auction, he smiled and said: 'That's progress, I suppose.' Henry received many farming awards, and was presented with an MBE in March 1956 in recognition of his hard work and services to the community. After Henry's death his wife, Caroline, remained at the farm until 1970, after which the farm buildings were soon pulled down.

Hay balers take a well-deserved rest, in the summer of 1897.

Even though the sun was shining down strongly, they still kept well-wrapped up.

In the distance John Fenwick Wilson (sitting to the left) looks on as Marden Farm work horses are shown off to the camera. But it wasn't all work and no play for the horses. They were always immensely popular with the Wilson's children, who often liked to ride the horses and help take care of them. Many of the animals were given affectionate nicknames.

It is remarkable to think that today rows and rows of houses stand where this farm land once was. After the Second World War, new housing estates became exceedingly important and the radical building programme in the 1950s reflected that. It's sad in one respect, though, that the field you see here has gone forever. Part of the joy of living in Tynemouth and Cullercoats during that period was the vast open spaces and gorgeous, fresh, salty sea air wafting well inland. All that and no traffic pollution!

Feeding the chickens. These two ladies names are unknown, but they were believed to have worked on Marden Farm from about 1895 onwards.

There were different designs for pails. These ones were used for feeding the chickens, the others for milking.

Hay baling, *c.* 1898. The majority of farmhands lived close by. They would make their daily trek to work in the small hours of the morning, ready for a sixteen-hour day. It was hard work and the pay was low compared with today's standards, but they were loyal to the Wilsons. A few, like the maids and Jack Potts the foreman (seen opposite), actually lived on the farm.

Potato planting, *c.* 1898. In the distance is St George's church, just off Tynemouth's Grand Parade. The women dealt mainly with the potato planting and gathering. On the surface the work was seemingly effortless, but the constant bending meant for backbreaking labour.

Jack Potts was foreman at
Marden Farm from 1894 to 1920.
He is pictured here in 1905.

Milkmaids are ready for a hard day's work in 1903.

One of the Marden Farm sheep dogs receives some attention in 1904.

Is this visitor to Marden Farm a boy or is it a girl? This photograph has mystified many, including living relatives of John and Henry Fenwick Wilson, who aren't totally sure. It was customary in 1905, when this photograph was taken, for little boys to wear 'dresses'. The apparent short hair could be misleading, as the hair may be tied up in the hat. As to whether the visitor pushes a pram or a wheelbarrow and whether it contains a doll or a teddy bear – it's up to the reader to make their own decision.

Children of friends of the Wilson family play at Marden Farmhouse in 1907. They are believed to be members of the Potts family, though were of no relation to Jack Potts.

The same children enjoy a game on a child's horse.

Two children enjoy a picnic during the summer of 1900. The girl is Evelyn Wilson, daughter of John Fenwick Wilson.

John Fenwick Wilson (seated to the left) enjoys a picnic with family and friends, during a drive around the farm fields, c. 1919. John Fenwick Wilson was in the fortunate position of being able to afford one of the first cars to be seen on the roads of the North East.

A mass of soldiers pose for a group photograph in 1915. Some of them hold musical instruments, including trombones and trumpets.

Soldiers get to grips with some farm duties, 1916. Here they are pictured at the important task of washing their vests and long johns!

Soldiers on parade with their horses in 1915.

Another parade in 1915, but this time in the background Marden Farmhouse is visible.

Proudly standing to attention. A soldier is pictured in full uniform at the side of Marden Farm in 1916.

A fine filly is shown off to camera in 1915.

Looking directly into the eyes of a soldier, *c.* 1915.

A family gathering at Marden Farm, *c.* 1912. From left to right, back row: Henry Fenwick Wilson (son), Evelyn Wilson (daughter), T.E Rowell. Front: -?-, the familiar figure of John Fenwick Wilson (wearing a bowler hat), Norah Wilson (daughter), Elizabeth Wilson (John's wife), -?-.

Two

Leading into Tynemouth

Leading on to Tynemouth's Grand Parade from Beverley Terrace, Cullercoats. The year is 1902. An open-topped No. 10 tram slowly travels along in the direction of the Plaza. On the front of the tram there is an advertisement for 'Cluny Whisky'. St Georges church is in the background.

Wil Hunter's popular entertainment troupe, Tynemouth Pierrots, in full costume in 1907.

Percy Park Road, *c.* 1922. We are looking towards the junction of Front Street, Manor Road, and Tynemouth Road, leading to North Shields.

Spittledene Tynemouth.

Spittledene, Tynemouth, 1902.

Front Street West, Tynemouth, *c.* 1904. In view is Queen Victoria's monument.

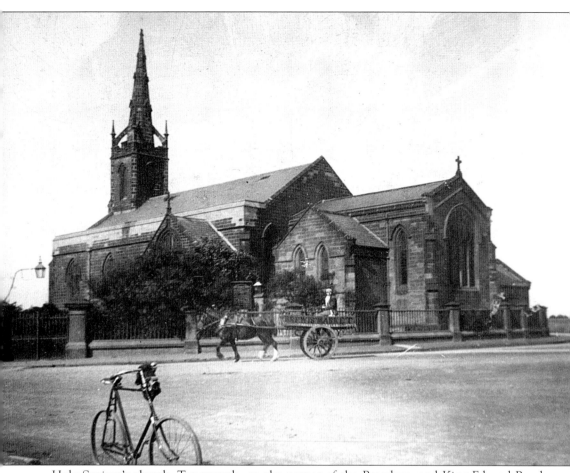

Holy Saviour's church, Tynemouth, on the corner of the Broadway and King Edward Road, March 1900. A sign of the times – a bike is left unlocked at the roadside, the owner obviously had no worries about disappearing before he returned. A well established nineteenth-century place of worship, Holy Saviour's church is still present today, managing effortlessly to blend in with its twentieth-century surroundings. Reflecting the vast increase in road traffic, a roundabout now exists to the right of the position of the horse and cart.

A drawing of the Tynemouth Priory, as it looked in 1450.

Tynemouth's distinguished monument to Queen Victoria, viewed looking down Front Street, c. 1930. A listed monument, it remains a constant fixture to the present day. The now faded inscription reads: 'Erected by public subscription to the memory of our late beloved Queen Victoria by the inhabitants of the borough of Tynemouth.' It was officially unveiled on 25 October 1902.

Grand Hotel, Tynemouth.

The Grand Hotel, Tynemouth's Grand Parade, *c.* 1882. This hotel was built in 1872. In 1932, top cinema comedy duo Laurel and Hardy paid a call to the hotel. Stan Laurel was born in Ulverston on 16 June 1890, but had moved to North Shields in 1897, where he lived until 1901. Having spent many years seeking and finding film fame and fortune in America, his visit was a treasured home-coming.

Tynemouth Cliffs, Pier, Castle and Priory, as seen from Percy Gardens, *c.* 1910.

A queue waits patiently for Ralph Pigg's grocery shop and post office to open, in the region of East Street, Tynemouth, *c.* 1886.

The impressive row of houses known as Percy Gardens, Tynemouth, c. 1913. When they were first sold their buyers had to be wealthy people. As Percy Gardens looks out to sea these properties have always been in great demand, but still today they are basically reserved for the advantaged only. Some of the properties have been converted into flats, thus offering the average wage earner an opportunity to live there. Enclosed within a private road there are gates at either end. The picture you see here is exactly as Percy Gardens looks today.

Front Street East, looking towards the direction of the Priory, Tynemouth, in 1900.

Percy Gardens, *c.* 1920. A rare sight in those days, a parked car!

Percy Gardens, c. 1910, as seen from the other end of the road. Behind is Sea Banks.

Shoppers in Front Street, Tynemouth, c. 1893. To the right is the Percy Arms public house. By the 1930s, the corner shop had established itself as Robson's ladies and gents hairdresser. It also sold cigarettes.

The procession of cars known as 'the village trip' travel along Front Street in September 1925. To the left is the Cumberland Arms, which is one of the oldest surviving public houses in the country. To the right of that is Walter Wilson's store.

The village trip, 1927. From left to right are the Bath Hotel, Arthur Dagg – which was established in 1857 as a dispensing and photographic chemist, M. Dalziel, the post office, T. Willits store, the motor garage and stables, and The Salutation Hotel which was licensed at the time in the name of Thomas Mitchell. The Salutation has been a feature in Front Street since the late 1600s.

A rare glimpse into the lives of the affluent who lived in Tynemouth, c. 1910. This was one of the many well furnished rooms at 58 Percy Park. The property was once the residence of the Wilsons of Marden farm. For them the house was a comfortable and private retreat from the, sometimes hectic, daily duties of running a farm. Every possession in this room would now be an antique, although in those days some of them were newly made! The framed pictures hanging on the walls show seaside scenes of Tynemouth and Cullercoats. Perhaps one or two readers now own some of the items in the photograph – get your magnifying glass out!

Front Street, *c.* 1894. Horse and carts and barrows were the main form of transportation for dealers.

Front Street is more or less deserted, *c.* 1910. The drinking fountain in the foreground was erected in 1861.

Sea Banks, Tynemouth, looking towards Percy Gardens, *c.* 1905. To the left is Lancaster's Café, where a boy can be seen delivering fresh bread and rolls. To the right, a rival refreshment room, Thomason's. In an attempt perhaps to get one over on the competition there is a notice stating 'schools and parties catered for'.

The Grand Hotel, *c*. 1920. Some children can be seen near to the front entrance as well as by the downstairs bay window.

The Gibraltar Rock, formerly the Gibraltar Hotel, East Street in 1968. Like The Salutation, it has a long history, dating back for more than two centuries.

PARK HOTEL, TYNEMOUTH. 13178.

The Tynemouth Park Hotel, just off Grand Parade, was built in 1938, and officially opened in 1939. Here it is seen around 1940. Over the past twenty years various extensions have been built on. It continues to be successful in business today.

ROAD
CLOSED

LANDSLIP AT TYNEMOUTH. 1913.

Chaos was caused in Tynemouth when a 'landslip' occurred in 1913. The nearby road was closed off, as can be seen from the notice at the top left of this scene.

Three
Rogues' Gallery
and Fishwives

Around the turn of the century, hundreds of mug shots were taken at Tynemouth and Cullercoats, of people who had fallen on the wrong side of the law. Both young and old, they had committed, in general, minor crimes of theft, but the punishment could be very harsh.

The following photographs provide an absorbing insight into the kind of dishonest people whom the police eventually caught up with. They were not villains in the true sense of the word, but might instead be described as victims of the hardship of their times. Tynemouth sometimes comes under the banner of North Shields, which explains why most of the people are seen holding slates bearing that name. Will Cunningham is pictured here on 23 March 1903, he was arrested and charged with larceny (theft of personal goods).

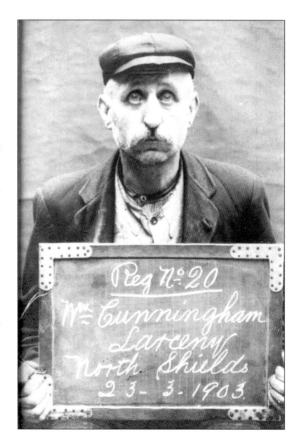

Just a boy, but already in trouble with the law. David Gavin can't have been more than thirteen years old when this photograph was taken on 27 February 1899. David was charged with larceny, but who knows what his exact punishment would have been. Any crime, no matter how seemingly infinitesimal, was met with a severe sentence. David may have only stolen a loaf of bread but he could have expected a long stay in confinement or the workhouse. Children did not have the protection they receive today. Being below the age of criminal responsibility did not exist as a defence for David, nor was there any scheme to provide him with a solicitor. Many years would pass before the law would show clemency to children.

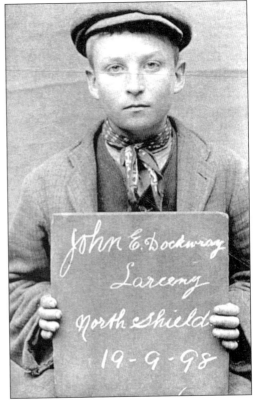

This is another teenager, John E. Dockwray, who was charged with larceny. He is pictured on 19 September 1898. John looks about sixteen years old in this mug shot. Mortality rates were fairly high in 1898, though if he had survived until 1914 he may well have ended up fighting in the First World War and a high percentage of those men who left to fight never returned. All in all it was not perhaps the best era in which to live. One wonders what happened to John and others like him.

Crime was not a male preserve; Susan Joice, seen here on 18 August 1903, was charged with larceny. Judging by her clothes, Susan may have been a fishwife. Was she married at the time? Did she have children? Her imprisonment, if found guilty, would almost certainly have serious repercussions for her family. Without their mother and a solid home base the children too may have turned to crime – a vicious circle.

Annie Anderson was well known for her frequent brushes with the law in and around North Shields, Tynemouth and Cullercoats. Here she is on 25 August 1903, charged with larceny.

Henry Wilson Charles Murray was charged with false pretences, 24 April 1903. His was one of the few ethnic-looking faces around at the time. However, with a name such as his, he was definitely British and not from foreign shores; though his family tree undoubtedly originated elsewhere. North Shields police station no longer recognises the validity of the charge of false pretences, as its interpretation is too open.

An obviously unhappy Alice Caush was charged with larceny, 31 October 1903. The surname Caush is rare to the area, with only a few people sharing that surname in the entire North East telephone directory. It seems likely therefore that one of those Caush's that is listed is in fact a direct descendant of Alice.

Putting on a look of defiance Joseph G. Roberts was charged with larceny, 18 July 1903. Joseph would have been born around 1870. It's unlikely that he saw front line action in the First World War, as he would by then have been well into his forties.

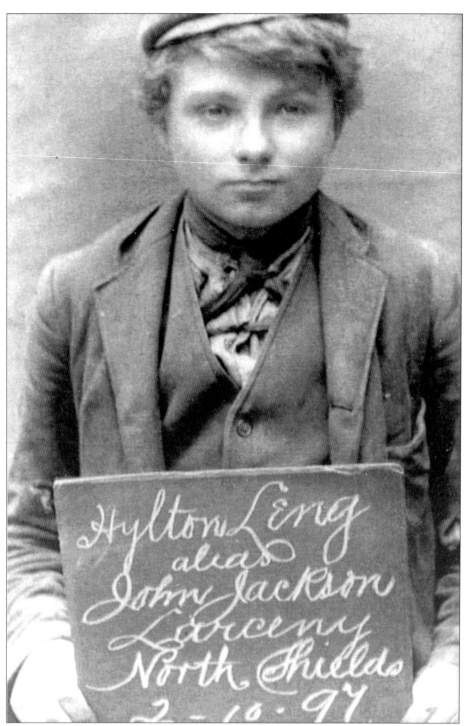

This teenager is Hylton Leng. He was also known by the alias John Jackson. John or Hylton was charged with larceny on 2 October 1897. John, unlike all the others on a charge, has the faintest of smiles on his lips. Maybe he was sure he wouldn't be convicted. John obviously recognised the freedom and anonymity that the use of an alias could bring him.

Annie Lisle is laden with baskets, *c.* 1922. Annie's husband, John Lisle, was founder of Cullercoats' Fisherman's Mission

Cullercoats fisher girls, *c*. 1895.
Such characters have long been the
inspiration for countless plays, short stories
and poems. They remain the object of
fascination and respect.

Waiting for the boats to come in, Cullercoats Bay, *c*. 1895. On a bleak looking day, fishwives
stand huddled together, warmly wrapped up in their familiar funereal black, long frocks and
shawls. Retirement with a state pension wasn't an option so many of them worked on into old
age.

Janey McCully sets up her crab stall in Cullercoats during the 1920s. Janey came from a fishing family. Her face should be easily recognisable to the older generation, who may well recall buying crabs from her stall.

A woeful Cullercoats fisher lass, *c.* 1900. The empty basket is strategically positioned for us to see.

Cullercoats fisher girls look out to sea, waiting for their menfolk to return with the day's catch, *c.* 1900.

Fishwives prepare to sell their wares in Cullercoats in 1897.

Boiling crabs in Back Row, Cullercoats. Bell Jefferson is on the left with Janey McCully on the right, in the 1920s.

This is the young Lizzie Taylor, who continued running her crab stall right into old age. Lizzie appeared in various seaside postcards of Cullercoats. This particular photograph was taken in Front Street, around 1926, as Lizzie is about to head off to market.

A hive of activity as usual – Front Street, Cullercoats in 1927. Pictured from left to right are: William Taylor, -?-, the ever-present Lizzie Taylor, David Taylor, -?-, Bell Jefferson.

Cullercoats fisher lasses talking together, c. 1890.

Front Street, Cullercoats, 1930. Lizzie Taylor is on the left, and Bell Jefferson on the right.

Four

Tynemouth Plaza
and Coast

The Tynemouth Plaza, *c.* 1910. The boating lake and park are visible to the left. In later years houses would be built on much of the land.

The Plaza in all its glory, as seen from the boating lake, on a dull day in January 1905. While only one interior photograph of the Plaza is included among the following pictures, there are several exterior pictures showing the well known landmark from around the early part of the this century. It reigned supreme for nearly 120 years. Unfortunately, the Plaza was the victim of a raging fire in 1996, which gutted the property. Shortly afterwards it was, sadly, demolished. The Plaza Ballroom, or 'The Aquarium' or 'Tynemouth Palace' as it was also known, was erected during 1877 and 1878 at a cost of £82,000. This was an immense amount of money in those days, and, like London's Millennium Dome, it had a long way to go when it was first designed to convince people it was worth the expense. Indeed, travel writer William Weaver Tomlinson wasn't happy about it. In 1893, he had remarked that The Aquarium was a 'white elephant which although twice sold had never been remunerative as a place of entertainment.' True at the time, but it cannot be denied that the Plaza was a spectacular building. It had been constructed originally with a glass roof, under which was contained an aquarium. There was a bar, refreshment compartments and an ice rink. In later years, the Plaza was used as a theatre and for other entertainment. Towards the end of its days, many people lamented the fact that this huge Victorian building had been left to slowly decline over the years. Its main purpose during the early 1990s was as a down-market amusement arcade.

Tynemouth Palace interior shot, taken at a time when it was being used as a theatre, *c*. 1920.

Here we see the now renamed Plaza Ballroom from the boating lake and park, *c*. 1977.

A sparse turnout at the Tynemouth Palace, flying the flag, *c.* 1895.

Tynemouth Park, *c.* 1898. The boating lake is to the right, and beyond that is the Plaza. St George's church is in the distance, but there is no Park Hotel or houses like there are today.

A rarely seen view of the boating lake and park, from the top of the Plaza, then known as the Tynemouth Palace, *c*. 1896.

226 Tynemouth Swimming Bath

Tynemouth's famous outdoor swimming pool, in the late 1920s. It opened on 30 May 1925 and proved hugely popular with holidaymakers who liked to swim in the seawater, but were a bit cautious of the waves.

Tynemouth Long Sands, 1912. In view is the tall spire of St George's church. This photograph was taken when the summer season was coming to an end, probably in late August. A few weeks earlier and this stretch of beach would no doubt have been packed – like the photograph below.

Try counting the people on Tynemouth Long Sands, c. 1892! Something, perhaps a spell of good weather, had obviously encouraged people to take a trip to the seaside.

A cart is pulled down Tynemouth Banks, *c*. 1895. Scottish holidaymakers made Tynemouth, Cullercoats and Whitley Bay their own as they mingled with locals enjoying the amusements, the sun, the sand and the sea. Crossing the border from Scotland was a considerable trip, so they'd make the most of their stay by taking up residence in the hotels and bed and breakfast accommodation available.

ON TYNEMOUTH SANDS.

The donkey rides were very popular at the time of this photograph, *c*. 1920.

Taking a stroll along Tynemouth Grand Parade, *c.* 1900.

Tynemouth Pier, *c.* 1910. The rail track can clearly be seen to the left of the picture.

An interesting painting from about 1820, shows how Tynemouth waters could sometimes be crammed with boats and ships, all afloat (and hopefully managing to avoid each other) upon the choppy sea.

Tynemouth Haven and Pier, c. 1907. This is an old postcard – and an unusual choice of location, it has to be said. Mainly postcards of the area focus on characters such as fishwives, or on buildings and streets – essentially on the popular areas of a holiday resort. This one is far from picturesque!

The entrance to the river Tyne and beach at Tynemouth, *c.* 1910.

King Edward Bay, *c.* 1930. To the right are the shadowy figures of the priory and castle.

Some things don't seem to change with the passing decades. The ruins of the priory and castle in August 1890 look more or less the same as they do today.

Tynemouth North Pier in 1895. A well-to-do family take a stroll in the fresh air. The priory is in clear view.

Tynemouth's North Pier, again in 1895, but this time seen from a different angle. The small train to the right was used for carrying coal.

Children at play on Tynemouth rocks, during a summer in the 1920s.

The Tynemouth Plaza and sands, 1911. The beach is packed with activity, from the children's swings and slides in the background to the bathing huts and holidaymakers in the foreground.

Tynemouth paddling (swimming) pool, c. 1932. Holidaymakers focus their attention on the fountain.

Tynemouth Collingwood Monument in all its magnificence, c. 1900.

Looking onto Tynemouth Long Sands in the late 1920s. The two ladies on the left, towels in hands, look all set for a day's sunbathing.

The banks of Tynemouth, in the 1890s. The large house on the Grand Parade, to the left of St George's church, has long since been demolished.

Tynemouth Long Sands in 1920. With the tide out, fathers, mothers and their children search the rocks for whelks. It was free and tasty fare, but the whelks weren't – and still aren't – always easy to find!

A solitary bathing carriage is pulled ashore onto Tynemouth sands, in 1904.

Skimming stones on Tynemouth Long Sands, October 1910. This gentleman was a friend of the Wilsons of Marden Farm.

Tynemouth, as seen from the priory, early 1960s. Looking up Front Street, the Gibraltar Rock Hotel is to the right, with the drinking fountain just off centre. The old car park, familiar for many years, has now gone. A huge building has taken its place, now blocking the wonderful view once appreciated by home owners in its vicinity.

Tynemouth Promenade and the outdoor bathing pool have attracted the crowds, *c.* 1930. The Grand Hotel is to the right.

The entrance to Tynemouth Harbour, *c.* 1930.

A stream of smartly dressed people walk along Tynemouth Pier, *c*. 1898.

The Tynemouth of old was always a most popular resort with the upper classes. However, as flights abroad became less expensive and more frequent, the wealthier visitors started to take their holidays in glamorous resorts abroad. The void left behind was filled by working-class families.

Disaster struck in 1905 when Tynemouth Pier was damaged.

Life was difficult for the lighthouse crew, who, without the pier, could only get to and from the lighthouse in a boat.

Tynemouth's famous outdoor swimming pool in July 1954.

Tynemouth Plaza, 1915. There are no motor vehicles to be seen, which meant that, in general, cycling on the road was safe. Recourse to the pavement for cyclists was therefore unnecessary.

A packed Tynemouth Long Sands, during the summer of 1922.

End of an era. It's 1996 and the Tynemouth Plaza has been gutted by fire. The decision is made to reluctantly pull down the whole building. After demolition, barren land was all that remained. Tynemouth will undoubtedly never see the like of this unique structure again.

Five
Cullercoats Inland

Davy Taylor and Son, makers and repairers of fishing nets, at Brown's Buildings, Front Street, Cullercoats, c. 1922. Brown's Buildings were erected sometime around 1836, and looked from the front like a typical row of fishermens' cottages. However, on closer inspection they were said to be 'nicely furnished', with ornate fireplaces.

Front Street, Cullercoats, 1906. The big building to the left of the cottages is the Ship Hotel (or Ship Inn), which was built in 1746. It was pulled down during the 1970s, when much of Front Street was demolished.

Possibly Back Row, Cullercoats, c. 1902. Regrettably, nothing now remains of these cottages.

Bank Top, Cullercoats, 1890s. To the right is the Watch House. The road where the two ladies are standing leads up what is now John Street. Commercial 'enterprise' saw the row of houses nearest to the left turned into amusement arcades and a fish shop.

Monks Haven, Beverley Terrace, Cullercoats, 1935. This was once the residence of Sir James Knott, the man who bestowed the money necessary to build Knott's flats in North Shields.

A sketch of Front Street, Cullercoats, in 1893. The Watch House is in the distance.

Cullercoats, as it appeared nearly two centuries ago, in 1820.

Identifying the exact location of this row of houses has proved difficult. It is definitely in the region of Front Street, Cullercoats. The picture was taken in the mid-1970s, just as the bulldozers were knocking down much of old Cullercoats. Looking to the left, we see that the house next door has already been pulled down. Such was the immediacy of the house demolition, pot plants were still present in the window and the curtains and net curtains were still hanging.

Selling crabs in Front Street, Cullercoats, *c.* 1947. In the background is the Fisherman's Mission. Lizzie Taylor is pictured on the left and Alan Scott is on the far right.

Huddleston Street, Cullercoats, looking towards Whitley Road in 1968. In the distance, to the right, is St Margaret's Methodist church.

The First World War is over. August 1919 saw a series of victory celebrations. This one was held in the grounds of St George's church, Cullercoats. The lady on the back row, third from left, is Sarah Sabiston. Second row, far left, is famous fishwife Polly Donkin. On the front row, far left, are Canon Fry and Emily Sabiston (Sarah's sister). Sarah later married and became Mrs Taylor, the wife of Bart Taylor, harbour master and beach superintendent at Cullercoats (see pp 103 and 115).

Beverley Terrace, Cullercoats, *c.* 1900. When they built these houses, they thought *big*. Not only were the rooms huge and the ceilings high, but the original skirting boards measured nearly three feet tall! The majority had, in addition, spacious underground cellars. To the right is Cullercoats Bay. A horse with cart and a tram travel in the direction of Tynemouth.

Looking down Station Road from John Street, Cullercoats, *c.* 1920. At the bottom is Cullercoats railway station. To the right is The Cosy Café, owned by J.W. Walton. A sign written in chalk reads: 'Ice cream today'. The café later became a betting shop.

Cullercoats viewed from a north-easterly point, c. 1910.

Huddleston Street, Cullercoats, in 1969. The bulldozers were to move in a few years later.

Cullercoats, as seen from the north side, *c.* 1920.

44301. Cullercoats. The Gardens.

The clement weather brings everyone out in their Sunday best to take a stroll past 'the gardens' on Cullercoats seafront, Beverley Terrace, *c.* 1898.

309. CULLERCOATS

The magnificent doorway to the left of centre is the entrance to The Bay Hotel, Cullercoats. It was originally called The Huddleston Hotel, but after being enlarged and renovated, the name was changed. Probably its most famous visitor was the celebrated American artist Winslow Homer, who, in 1880, stayed for a brief time at the hotel. He had sought the 'tranquillity' of an old English seaside village, a chance to relax and paint the scenes discernible from his bedroom window. He was captivated by Cullercoats and its people, and much of the work created while he was in residence bears testimony to his feelings about the area. As with the majority of public houses in Tynemouth, The Bay Hotel remains today as one of the last great watering holes in the North East.

Flooding in what is now known as Eksdale Terrace, Cullercoats, June 1924. To the rear is the junction between Margaret Road and John Street. Top left, but beyond the picture, is where the Fisherman's Mission was built seven years later in 1931.

The Newcastle Arms, Front Street, Cullercoats, 1972. The property might have survived Hitler's bombs but it couldn't escape the developers who knocked down what should have been a listed building.

Beverley Terrace, Cullercoats, *c*. 1898.

Front Street, Cullercoats, *c*. 1910.

St Margaret's Methodist church, Cullercoats, on the corner of Margaret Road and Whitley Road, 1988.

Gate to nowhere. Like most of 'old' Cullercoats, St Margaret's followed a sad trend in being demolished in 1990, much to the disapproval of local residents. The site lay derelict for a few years before modern flats were built there.

St George's church, Cullercoats, *c.* 1900.

To the right is Dial House, Cullercoats, *c.* 1930. Two men are just visible, leaning on the fence and looking out to sea.

Huddleston Street, *c.* 1912. Cullercoats residents had, at that time, many and varied shops to choose from. Today the supermarket reigns supreme, with consumers expecting to be able to fulfil all their shopping needs in one go.

Back Row, Cullercoats, in the 1890s. This is probably Sparrow Hall which was built by Thomas Dove during 1681 and '82. It acquired its name because the local fisher-folk had confused the figure of a dove carved on the finial which surmounted the east gable end, with that of a sparrow. Hence, Sparrow Hall.

The now demolished Back Row, Cullercoats, seen in December 1969. Bell Storey was a general dealer who had this shop for many years.

Back Row, Cullercoats, once more in 1969, but this time viewed from a different angle.

Cullercoats abattoir, Huddleston Street, c. 1924. It saw a 'great escape' in 1933 when one of the cattle broke loose. The intrepid beast managed to make it to Cullercoats railway station but was caught in the nick of time by an employee of the abattoir, just as the cow made a vain attempt to board a train!

The Queen's Head Inn, Front Street, Cullercoats, 1990. This pub dates back at least a couple of centuries and continues to flourish today.

Cullercoats Rocket Brigade, 1905. Members and bystanders look on excitedly as a rocket blasts off!

Workers, consisting of painters and joiners, take a 'break' in Cullercoats, 1926.

A family day out, in the 1930s. The man far left is Albert Lisle, son of John Lisle, founder of Cullercoats Fisherman's Mission. The Lisles were a large and legendary family, who made a substantial contribution to the Cullercoats' community of old (see pp 96 and 97).

Six
Buildings of Distinction

The Fisherman's Mission. The original Fisherman's Mission was based at this shop in Front Street, Cullercoats. Here, children and two adults enjoy a sing-a-long, around 1920. The banner reads: 'Cullercoats Mission Schools Sunday: God Bless Our School.'

John Lisle was founder of the Cullercoats Fisherman's Mission. Here he is in thoughtful mood, binoculars in hands, gazing out to sea, around 1922. The mission was under the leadership of Mr Albert Lisle – John Lisle's son.

Blind Mrs G.T. Bodden lays a foundation stone for the new Cullercoats Fisherman's Mission and Methodist church, in February 1931. It was officially opened in September of that same year by Mrs Thompson Hall, of Newcastle upon Tyne.

Cullercoats Fisherman's Mission and Methodist church, Front Street, 1933.

The Dove Marine Laboratory and The Salt Water Baths in Cullercoats Bay, summer 1897. In clear view are The Marine Laboratory 'hut' and Salt Water Baths. The lifeboat house is to the right, and the Watch House is just above it. This is a particularly fine photograph, there is so much going on. Note the activity to the top left – a workman holds a ladder while another climbs up it. The original Dove Marine Laboratory building – there have been two – was constructed under the auspices of the Northumberland Sea Fisheries Committee, and was officially opened on Thursday 21 October 1897. The laboratory exterior was nothing more than a characterless wooden hut next to the Salt Water Baths, which had been erected in Cullercoats Bay around 1807 by a gentleman called Richard Armstrong. On 9 April 1807 Mr Armstrong announced that he had made considerable improvements to the initial design of his salt water baths, which were positioned in an area where 'no fresh water could mix with the sea water and weaken its strength.' The Salt Water Baths were refilled every tide so as to avoid 'infection'. Inside were four bathrooms, each with a 'dressing room'. The purpose of the Marine Laboratory, as outlined in 1897, was to undertake scientific and systematic studies into the Northumberland coast fishery, with the long-term aim of furthering its prosperity.

Seven years on, it's March 1904 and fire has destroyed both the Marine Laboratory and Salt Water Baths.

Summer 1904. First on the list to be pulled down was the Marine Laboratory hut. Demolition of the Salt Water Baths soon followed.

September 1908. The new Marine Laboratory has just opened, thanks to the generosity of a local benefactor, Mr W.H. Huddleston, who named the three-storey brick building in memory of his ancestor, Eleanor Dove. The Dove family were, at the time, well known locally. In the last ninety years, the Dove Marine Laboratory has flourished as a major centre of research in the region. The accumulation of knowledge on the local plants and animals means that the coast's natural history is now among the best known in the world. The staff of the Dove Marine Laboratory now look forward to the exciting scientific marine challenges that the twenty-first century will doubtless bring.

Seven

Lifeboat Heroes
and Fisherman

Decorated Coastguard Hoare, who became legendary for his heroism.

Coxswain Robert 'Scraper' Smith set out with volunteers in a lifeboat on a bleak, stormy Saturday night on 1 November 1914, to the wreck of a hospital ship called *The Rohilla*, which had crashed on rocks at Whitby. Robert Smith, along with his brave volunteers, saved fifty lives.

Robert 'Scraper' Smith with a group of fishwives.

Bart Taylor was born on 1 August 1894. He was harbour master and beach superintendent for forty years at Cullercoats. For much of that time, he was second cox in the Cullercoats lifeboat, long before motorization was introduced. Bart hit the newspaper headlines in 1942 when the Norwegian vessel *Bergenfjord* was mined off the Tyne. He was awarded King Haakon's Medal and the National Lifeboat Institution Vellum for the rescue of the chief officer. Curiously though, the actual deed that won him recognition was not aboard the Cullercoats boat, but on the Tynemouth lifeboat. Bart, who died on 4 October 1979, at the ripe old age of eighty-five, has long since gone down in history as one of the 'grand old men' of Cullercoats.

Bart Taylor (left) with his wife Sarah by his side, along with friends, on Cullercoats Bay, in the 1920s. St George's church is behind them.

The Duke of Northumberland gave Cullercoats' lifeboat house its first lifeboat on 6 September 1852. This is a sketch from the 1930s, showing choppy seas at Cullercoats. A group of men and a boy look on anxiously as the lifeboat crew attempt to save the crew of a boat in distress.

This old sea dog was a well known fixture of Tynemouth and Cullercoats. His name was Andrew Taylor.

Cullercoats' lifeboat men race to answer the alert in 1933.

This painting dates back to about 1894. It shows a worried mother and family standing on the edge of Cullercoats Pier, as they all reach out to a young child who has just been saved from a vessel in distress. The waves crash around them. The painting perfectly depicts both the time and the moment.

Crowds gather beside the Watch House as Cullercoats lifeboat is manoeuvred into place, *c*. 1920.

Dawn breaks around Cullercoats waters, *c*. 1928.

A work of art entitled 'Perils of the Deep', painted by Owen Dalziel in 1888.

Members of Cullercoats Lifeboat, *c.* 1930.

Tynemouth Volunteer Life Brigade Quarters, *c.* 1975. The building was established in 1864. The monument to Admiral Lord Collingwood, in the centre of the picture, was erected in 1845. It was designed by John Dobson and sculptured by John Gorden Lough. Admiral Lord Collingwood was second in command to Nelson in the battle of Trafalgar.

Tynemouth lifeboat on display, *c.* 1920.

CULLERCOATS LIFEBOAT.

Cullercoats lifeboat and volunteers, *c.* 1900. The lifeboat house is to the right, and the Salt Water Baths are to the left.

The Lifeboat House. Cullercoats Bay.

Cullercoats lifeboat house in the 1890s.

The *Co-operator* No. 1 Lifeboat was a gift from the Co-operative Wholesale Society Limited, and was officially launched on Saturday 13 September 1884.

The Watch House, *c.* 1924. It was officially opened in October 1879 as a look-out point for the members of the Volunteer Lifeboat Brigade. It has been instrumental in saving countless lives.

Fishermen get their nets ready in Cullercoats Bay, 1928. This picture was taken from a collection of old lantern slides which were transferred onto photographic paper. A splendid snapshot, but alas the name of the boat, and those of her fishermen, remains unknown.

Eight
Schools and
Railway Stations

Cullercoats Junior School in John Street, *c.* 1930. Each child was given a reproduction of this photograph, which was taken home and proudly shown to 'mam and dad'. Few of the original photographs that make up this chapter survive today. However, the copies that remain afford us a charming glance as some of the children and teachers of yesteryear.

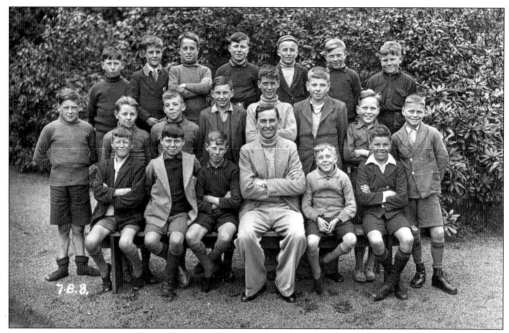

Members of Cullercoats School, John Street, *c.* 1938, on a trip to Newbiggin Hall Summer Camp. The trips were always hugely favoured by the children, as, for the majority, it was an opportunity to take their first journey outside their community and enjoy and learn about a different environment.

Members of the Cullercoats School sports team pose for a picture in 1938.

A group of girls from the John Street school, *c.* 1903. The girl in the second row, second from the right, has been identified as Sarah Sabiston, who can also be found on page 81, celebrating the end of the First World War. She later married and became Sarah Taylor.

Cullercoats Senior School, John Street, 1934.

Cullercoats Infants School, John Street, 1928. From left to right, back row: Colin Lisle, Kenny Barris, Eddie Wilson, M. Pearson, Raey Taylor, P. Harding. Third row up: George Storey, Jackie Logan, -?-, -?-, -?-, -?-. Second row: Robin Rigby, Billy Hyde, -?-, -?-, George Brunton, Brian Lisle. Bottom row: Ronnie Slater, Joe Brunton, -?-, -?-, -?-, Kenny Campbell.

Cullercoats School, John Street, 1935. One of the teachers poses with a group of children.

Cullercoats School, John Street, 1934. Pictured on the bottom row are Raey and Bart Taylor.

Heavy rainfalls caused a flood in 1903, temporarily causing havoc for commuters at Cullercoats railway station. The track leads to Whitley Bay, Monkseaton, and so on.

This is the view from the other side of the station. To the left is Marden Terrace. Travelling from the right over the bridge from Mast Lane and down Marden Avenue leads to Cullercoats seafront and Beverly Terrace. The large building to the top left has had many uses. It began as St Oswald's Diocesan Home for Waifs and Strays – in effect a girls' hostel. Then it became a naval hospital during the Second World War, and after that the YMCA. During the late 1980s, it was used to teach the unemployed skills to enable them to get back into work. It was recently demolished and replaced by comfortable flats.

Tynemouth station, 1897. In those days countless people would travel to the coast from Newcastle upon Tyne and surrounding areas. The station was built with that in mind, so the platforms were wide and long. As the years passed, Tynemouth as holiday resort lost out to places abroad.

The familiar foliage of Victorian times. Tynemouth station was commissioned and built in 1882 by the North Eastern Railway Company, surprisingly not as long ago as some people may think. The blueprint was designed by William Bell. The station went through a very rough patch during the 1970s, as it was left to slowly deteriorate, the paint flaked and vandalism was rife. A massive regeneration programme got underway in the 1980s and the station was given a new lease of life while still retaining its original Victorian features; it was renamed Tynemouth Metro Station.

Tynemouth station, *c.* 1900. The two smartly dressed ladies stand next to a booth selling tobacco. To the right, station ticket inspectors and porters chat to a group of passengers, some with children wearing deluxe bonnets.

Tynemouth in bloom, *c.* 1900. If you had taken a train to the right, you'd be travelling towards Whitley Bay, Monkseaton, leading to Newcastle upon Tyne. To the left, a different route to Newcastle, via North Shields. The plants and shrubs are all around the station platform, creating a wonderfully serene atmosphere. Vandalism was rare – if ever seen at all in 1900.

Work on the track gets underway in Tynemouth station. , pre-Metro days. The old trains had an agreeable style and efficiency about them. Unlike the modern trains running to and from the coast, they had interior toilets and overhead luggage compartments made from netting.

Porters pose for a photograph. Behind them is a Class 3242 North Eastern Railway train.

The exterior of Tynemouth station, *c.* 1980, before the restoration got underway.

Sadly, the neglect and vandalism are there for all to see. Objections to the state of Tynemouth station gathered pace and eventually the powers-that-be listened and acted to restore the station to its former glory. The 'Friends of Tynemouth Station' exists to provide historic information and organise meetings extolling the station's glorious past.

Nine

Scenes of Tynemouth
and Cullercoats

Cullercoats Pier in 1925. In view to the top left is the Watch House, and to the right, Dail House and Cliff House.

Looking inland from the end of Cullercoats Pier in 1900. A solitary fisherman casts his rod.

Beach and Bay, Cullercoats

Cullercoats Bay and sands, 1934. Two men chat together, while a Scottish piper is visible far left. This postcard was retrieved from a box of bric-a-brac – it's amazing what people throw out!

Huge waves crash on rocks just below Cliff House, *c.* 1925. Cliff House was built sometime around the early part of the 1700s.

Two boys and two girls climb the steep hill onto Bank Top, Cullercoats, *c.* 1922. To the left is Snaith's Café.

Looking towards Front Street, Tynemouth, from Manor Road, *c.* 1896. A few of the buildings on Huntingdon Place, to the right of the picture, belong to King's School for boys and girls. It was opened in 1864 and is to this day one of the region's leading fee-paying centres of education, offering a wide curriculum.

An interesting view of the sea at Cullercoats, taken from the Bay Hotel, in the 1920s. Scenes such as this one inspired the American artist Winslow Homer to pick up his brushes and paint some of his most well received works of art (see p. 85).

Various small boats are afloat on waters just off Cullercoats Bay, *c.* 1922.

Percy Street, Tynemouth, in 1972. This shows the property before it gained a new roof.

Cullercoats Bay, c. 1890. These visitors to the seaside are wearing a lot of clothes for a sunny day on the beach.

The Cliffs, Tynemouth.